Cold Case: Dinosaurs

by Gretchen McBride

PEARSON

Scott
Foresman

Editorial Offices: Glenview, Illinois • Parsippany, New Jersey • New York, New York
Sales Offices: Needham, Massachusetts • Duluth, Georgia • Glenview, Illinois
Coppell, Texas • Ontario, California • Mesa, Arizona

The World's Coldest Case

A paleontologist is like a detective investigating a "cold case," which is a mystery that has remained unsolved for such a long time that the trail has grown cold. The clues have become difficult to uncover. Paleontologists, or scientific detectives who specialize in prehistoric life, have been working hard for almost two centuries to uncover clues that will solve the cold case of the dinosaurs. But two hundred years is not a long time when the trail went cold millions of years ago. When scientists first began to study the bones and fossils left behind by these mysterious animals, they weren't sure what they were looking at.

Long Ago, but Not So Far Away...

When scientists talk about time, they use the term *geologic time*. We are currently in the Phanerozoic eon, which can be broken down into three eras. The Paleozoic era was the time of ancient life and ended about 245 million years ago. That was followed by the Mesozoic era. We are now in the Cenozoic era.

Eras are divided into periods. The oldest period of the Mesozoic era is the Triassic period. During the Triassic period, the first dinosaurs appeared. Following the Triassic period was the Jurassic period, after which came the Cretaceous period.

It is easier to use these terms than to number the millions of years that make up these time periods. In this book we will use these terms for prehistoric time that geologists and paleontologists use in their work. Looking at the chart on the facing page will help you become familiar with terms and learn how many years ago each period was. Find *mya* on the chart. This is a shorthand way of writing *million years ago*. So 65 mya means 65 million years ago.

Scientists believe that humans did not appear on Earth until about 1.87 million years ago. Think of all the different kinds of animals and plants that existed before then!

ERA	PERIOD	
Cenozoic Era (Age of Mammals) 65 mya (million years ago) through today	Quaternary Period (Age of Man) 1.8 mya to today	
	Tertiary Period 65 to 1.8 mya	Neogene Period 24 to 1.8 mya
		Paleogene Period 65 to 24 mya
Mesozoic Era (Age of Reptiles) 248 to 65 mya	Cretaceous Period 146 to 65 mya	
	Jurassic Period 208 to 146 mya	
	Triassic Period 248 to 208 mya	
Paleozoic Era 540 to 248 mya	Permian Period (Age of Amphibians) 280 to 248 mya	
	Carboniferous Period 360 to 280 mya	Pennsylvanian Period 325 to 280 mya
		Mississippian Period 360 to 325 mya
	Devonian Period (Age of Fishes) 408 to 360 mya	
	Silurian Period 438 to 408 mya	
	Ordovician Period 505 to 438 mya	
	Cambrian Period 540 to 505 mya	

Mass Extinction

A mass extinction is when large groups of plants or animals die off. When we think of a mass extinction, we usually think of the one that occurred at the end of the Cretaceous period, when most of the dinosaurs became extinct. There was also a dramatic extinction that occurred at the end of the Permian period, which directly preceded the Triassic period.

Scientists study fossil records to learn about the kinds of plants, animals, and insects that lived during certain time periods. The fossil records are made up of different remnants of life (bone, shells, etc.) that can be found in the rock layers, or strata, of Earth.

This cross-section of rock shows rock layers, or strata, where fossils from different time periods can be seen.

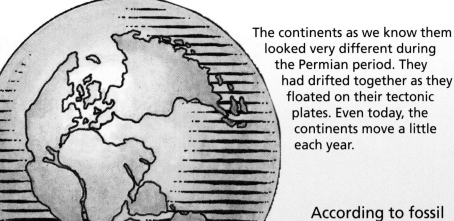

The continents as we know them looked very different during the Permian period. They had drifted together as they floated on their tectonic plates. Even today, the continents move a little each year.

According to fossil records, abundant animal life had developed in the Permian period, but nearly all of the marine invertebrate species (animals without spines) were wiped out, as were a majority of the land vertebrates (animals with spines). At the same time, there was an increase in the number and kinds of reptiles. There was also a change in the kinds of insects. Scientists think that this was all due to dramatic changes in the environment.

Early in the Permian period, icy glaciers covered extensive areas of land. Other areas had hot and dry desert climates. The continents were different from our present-day continents. By the middle of the Permian period the continents, which float on tectonic plates, had drifted together. The result was one massive continent called Pangaea, which means "all earth." Pangaea was surrounded by the world ocean, Panthalassa, and the Tethys Sea. In these waters were a few very small bodies of land.

By the beginning of the Triassic period, most of Pangaea had a hot, dry climate with seasons of monsoon rains. Over the course of the period, which lasted about 40 million years, the shallow ocean waters at the edge of Pangaea rose and large marine reptiles populated the shores.

On the Trail of the Earliest Dinosaurs

In the early 1800s, evidence of dinosaurs was turned up—literally—by a farm boy in Massachusetts. While plowing a field on his family's farm, Pliny Moody found pieces of sandstone with strange imprints on them. They turned out to be footprints. The footprints looked like a bird's, with three toes. Moody called the imprints the footprints of "Noah's Raven," because they made him think of the raven sent out from Noah's ark. It would be more than sixty years before the footprints would be recognized as those of a dinosaur, and it took even longer for scientists to figure out that they were from the Triassic period. The dinosaur was eventually named *Otozoum moodi*, in honor of the boy who found the first evidence of its existence.

Fossil footprints of dinosaurs are still found in New England, but skeletal remains are rare in that area.

The early dinosaur detectives mistook these footprints in stone for the footprints of giant birds. They had good reason to think of birds. Not only were the tracks three-toed, but they came from a bipedal creature, a creature that walked and ran on two legs.

A possible ancestor of the first dinosaurs was one of the "ruling reptiles," the *Lagosuchus*, a fast-moving predator of the early Triassic period that ran on two legs. Like this creature, the early dinosaurs of this time were often fast and bipedal. They were also small compared to the later, more famous giants of the Earth.

Very little is known about the early Triassic period because few fossils and skeletons have been found from that time period. That's why scientists were excited when the complete skeleton of an *Eoraptor* was found in Argentina.

Over the years, more and more clues to the mysterious world of the dinosaurs have been found in various places around the world. Let's look at a few of them.

Lagosuchus

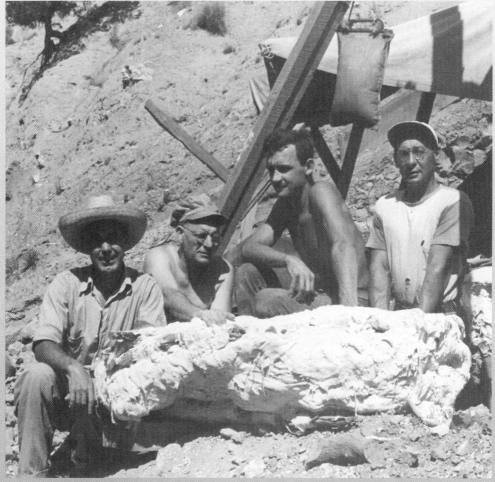

Ghost Ranch in the badlands of New Mexico was the site of a discovery that puzzled scientists.

Discovery at Ghost Ranch

A local legend about the ghost of a snake gave this place its name. Although that's just a ghost story, a rather surprising discovery was made at Ghost Ranch in 1947.

Paleontologists from the American Museum of Natural History (AMNH) explored the area because important dinosaur discoveries had been made there in the past. In the late 1800s David Baldwin, a private collector, found some **fragile**, hollow bones in a dried riverbed. He sent them back to the Yale College Museum in Connecticut, where they were identified as the bones of a small dinosaur weighing no more than seventy pounds. The newly discovered species was named *Coelophysis*, or "hollow form."

The team from the AMNH discovered a bone bed at Ghost Ranch as well. It seemed to be a mass grave of the dinosaur *Coelophysis*. The scientists wondered what had caused the dinosaurs to die together like that. One theory is that a herd may have been hunting together and were caught by a sudden natural disaster, such as a flash flood. Whatever the reason, the scientists made some important finds that helped them gain knowledge about the early dinosaurs.

Coelophysis

In the Valley of the Moon

In 1988 University of Chicago paleontologist Paul Sereno was in Argentina at a place known as the Valley of the Moon. He was on the trail of an early dinosaur, the *Herrerasaurus*, or "Herrera's lizard." It was named after the Argentinean artisan who found the first small **specimens** in 1958.

Sereno believed that finding skeletal remains of *Herrerasaurus*, thought to be one of the earliest of the dinosaurs, might answer some questions about the Triassic period. But paleontologists had been looking in this area for more than twenty-five years and had not turned up any significant fossils.

Even the National Science Foundation, the organization funding the exhibition, did not think his chances for success were great. Still, the possibility of uncovering a significant clue in the mystery of dinosaur evolution made the risk worthwhile.

However, in 1989, Sereno proved them all wrong with a spectacular discovery: a full skeleton of a *Herrerasaurus*. This find allowed him to determine what this early dinosaur had in common with other dinosaurs and what was different about it.

Herrerasaurus was approximately thirteen feet long and weighed more than seven hundred pounds. This dinosaur was bipedal. Since it stood on its hind legs, the forelegs of this meat-eater were free for grasping **prey**. Its teeth were of the sharpest kind, necessary for cutting through flesh. It also had unusually long and fang-like middle teeth. The *Herrerasaurus*'s jaw joint was more flexible than those of other dinosaurs. Once it wrapped that jaw around its prey, there was no escape. No doubt Paul Sereno and his team were glad they would not be facing a living "Herrera's lizard."

Herrerasaurus

Sereno was not finished investigating in the Valley of the Moon. He needed to find out just how old the skeleton was. To do this, he needed to find a perfect crystal of **volcanic** ash from the same area as the dinosaur remains for radiometric dating. A scientist can tell when a crystal was formed by analyzing the amount of radioactive material it contains. Once Sereno found a crystal he could date, he would know the approximate age of his find.

Sereno and a team member set out across the barren landscape to find the volcanic crystal they needed. Eventually, Sereno found the volcanic ash he was looking for. After the tests were completed back at the laboratory, they were certain that *Herrerasaurus* was a dinosaur of the middle Triassic period. The crystal came from the same place as the remains of the dinosaur, so the dinosaur had to be just as old as the crystal—about 228–230 million years old.

Valley of the Moon, Argentina

Cleaning an
Eoraptor skull

Catching a Thief

There would be another significant—if tiny—find on this mission to the Valley of the Moon. One of the members of Sereno's crew found the tiny skull of an animal. Digging deeper, its entire skeleton was found encased in rock. It turned out that this was a previously unknown dinosaur.

This newly discovered dinosaur was quite different from *Herrerasaurus*, with whom it shared the neighborhood. This dinosaur was small. It was just over three feet in length and probably weighed less than twenty-five pounds, about the size of a medium-sized dog. And yet, it was a meat-eater, which means it would have hunted its prey. It had long hind legs to run on and short forelegs to catch its prey. This dinosaur probably ate lizards and other small animals. Like *Herrerasaurus*, it lived during the late Triassic period, approximately 228 million years ago. It was named *Eoraptor*, which means "dawn thief."

Other Triassics Tracked Down

Before the complete skeleton of *Herrerasaurus* was found, little was known about this dinosaur. This is now true of *Mussaurus*. Much remains a mystery because a full adult skeleton has not yet been found. What have been found are very small skeletons, just eight inches in length, in a nest in Argentina. There was also an egg discovered that may have been that of a *Mussaurus*. Since the egg was so much smaller than a skeleton it seems that, similar to modern birds, these tiny dinosaurs might have remained in the nest until they had developed enough to be independent. This supports some scientists' theory that modern birds evolved from dinosaurs.

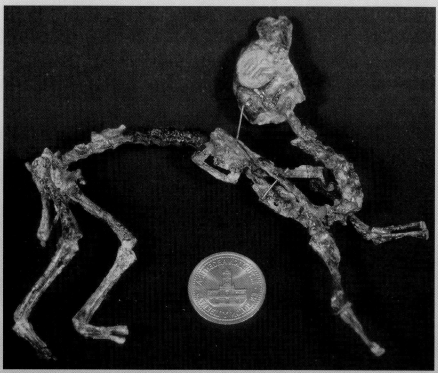

Mussaurus, or "mouse lizard"

Thecodontosaurus, or "socket-toothed lizard"

Bones of the *Thecodontosaurus* were first found in ancient caves in southwest England. The bones tell the tale of another relatively small dinosaur. This animal reached a length of eight feet. Based on the structure of its limbs, paleontologists think it may have walked on two legs most of the time, but it could also walk on four legs.

Its head was small, and its teeth suggest that it was omnivorous, eating both plants and animals. Some of the best specimens of *Thecodontosaurus* were destroyed when a museum in England was bombed during World War II. Luckily, more bones from this dinosaur have been found, and study of them continues.

Another unlikely victim of World War II, one of the best complete specimens of *Plateosaurus,* was destroyed in the bombing of Stuttgart, Germany. The skeleton had resided in the Stuttgart State Museum of Natural History. Luckily, paleontologists do have other examples for study.

This dinosaur was one of the most common of the Triassic period. Its bones are often found in large groups, which lead scientists to believe that they traveled in herds. Scientists theorize that herds of *Plateosaurus* may have died when they got stuck in the **treacherous** mud beneath the dried surface of watering holes shrunken by dry spells. Then their skeletons were buried by sand deposited when the rains came and the waters rose.

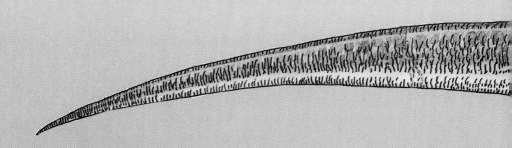

The bones tell scientists that the *Plateosaurus* was a fairly large dinosaur, about twenty-four feet long and weighing one and one-half tons. *Plateosaurus* was a herbivore.

This dinosaur was a quadruped, which means that it walked and ran on all four legs. However, it may have reared up on its hind legs to browse among taller plants. The animal's small head sat on a long neck.

A common feature of the *Plateosaurus* was its large nasal chamber. In other words, this dinosaur had a big nose. Scientists do not know what purpose this large nose served. Perhaps it gave the dinosaur a keen sense of smell, allowing it to smell a food source or a predator nearby. It is one of several mysteries still left unsolved in this cold case.

Plateosaurus, or "flat lizard"

Another dinosaur of South America, *Riojasaurus* was a larger dinosaur than *Plateosaurus*. It was first discovered in 1967. It weighed at least twice as much and may have grown as large as five tons. Its neck was somewhat shorter than the neck of *Plateosaurus*. Also a quadrapedal herbivore, *Riojasaurus* may at one time have stood on its hind legs and grasped vegetation with its "hands." These hands had a thumblike appendage tipped with a curved claw that was most likely used for defense.

Some scientists think that this dinosaur became larger and heavier over evolutionary time. As it did, it lost its ability to stand on its hind legs. This creature is thought to be the first of the giant dinosaurs that lived during the Jurassic period.

Riojasaurus, or "lizard from La Rioja"

As scientists study prehistoric creatures, the evidence is sometimes difficult to interpret. Often, scientists compare fossil discoveries to reptiles that are alive today in order to get clues about what dinosaurs were like. There are often disagreements about what the evidence shows.

One debate is about how dinosaurs moved. It seems likely that the giant quadrupeds were **sluggish** in their movements, but it appears that some of the dinosaurs moved quickly.

Another debate is whether or not some dinosaurs might have been **poisonous.** Most definitely were not, but a few fossils suggest that some may have been. Scientists point to the living Komodo dragon, a modern reptile with bacteria in its saliva that makes it poisonous. Who knows what the next big discovery will show us?

A Scientist's Job: Understanding Our World

You have probably heard little kids who constantly ask "Why?" It is a scientist's job to answer that question, as well as other big questions, about the way our world works. Scientists ask themselves those hard questions and are driven, at least in part, by their own curiosity to find the answers. We have seen that paleontologists are trying to answer questions about early animal life on our planet by studying fossils.

Paleontologists work in the field as well as in the lab. They search for clues to life that existed on this planet millions of years ago. By putting together bones and finding fossils, they are solving the puzzle of ancient animal life.

There are other fields of science that study the Earth in prehistoric times as well. Geologists, for instance, often go on expeditions with paleontologists to study the way the Earth was in the time of the dinosaurs. A geologist is a scientist who studies the history of the Earth as recorded in its rocks. Some geologists investigate possible explanations for how the dinosaurs became extinct.

The earthquakes that contribute to the movement of the continents, both now and in prehistoric times, are studied by scientists called *seismologists.* They work not just for the sake of knowing why an earthquake happens but also for the sake of saving people's lives in the future.

The next time you catch yourself thinking, "I wonder why that happens," know that you too may have the makings of a scientist. Maybe one day you will discover and name a dinosaur.

Glossary

fragile *adj.* easily broken, damaged, or destroyed; delicate.

poisonous *adj.* containing a dangerous substance; very harmful to life and health.

prey *n.* animal or animals hunted and killed for food by another animal.

sluggish *adj.* slow-moving; not active; lacking energy or vigor.

specimens *n.* samples.

treacherous *adj.* having a false appearance of strength, security, etc.; not reliable; deceiving.

volcanic *adj.* of or caused by a volcano.